M

D.H.

Selected an

This edition first published in Everyman Paperbacks in 1998
Selection, introduction and other critical apparatus
© J. M. Dent 1998

J. M. Dent
Orion Publishing Group
Orion House
5 Upper St Martin's Lane
London WC2H 9EA

Typeset by Deltatype Ltd, Birkenhead, Merseyside
Printed in Great Britain by
The Guernsey Press Co. Ltd, Guernsey C. I.

British Library Cataloguing-in-Publication
Data is available on request.

ISBN 0 460 87962 6

Contents

Note on the Author and Editor

D. H. LAWRENCE was born in 1885, to a mining family in Eastwood near Nottingham. The tension between his father's working-class manner and his mother's pretensions to gentility became the source of much of his early fiction. At the age of thirteen Lawrence won a scholarship to Nottingham High School and seemed set to fulfil some of his mother's ambition – but by 1901 he was working in a surgical appliance factory, and the same year went down with pneumonia. He was, for the rest of his life, scarcely free from ill-health and the threat of tuberculosis. In 1902 he became a pupil-teacher in Ilkeston and in 1906 a student at Nottingham University College – eventually becoming a qualified teacher at Davidson Road School in Croydon, where he worked from 1908 to 1911, until, once again, pneumonia forced him to quit. He had by this time begun to write seriously – his first published story had appeared in 1907 – and in his time at Croydon he completed his first two novels and began *Sons and Lovers*. His first poems were published in 1909, and he was quickly taken up by literary London, meeting, among others, Wells, Pound, Russell, Ford Madox Ford, Edward Garnett and Ottoline Morrell – and managed to feud with most of them at one time or another. His capacity for feuds probably killed off his most frequently aired ideal of a new communal society to be set up somewhere in the Americas – ironically, feuding was one of the problems such a society (to be named Ra Na Nim) was meant to solve. He never quite gave up on the idea but it existed only on the most *ad hoc* basis of being constantly surrounded by friends and fans.

In 1912 Lawrence met Frieda von Richthofen Weekley, daughter of a German baron, disciple of the new German erotic philosophy, and wife of one of his university tutors. She seduced him in less than twenty minutes, and in less than three months eloped with him – leaving her husband and three children. The rest of their life together was almost entirely peripatetic, tempestuous and financially uncertain – but it became, in a dozen forms, the subject of most of Lawrence's fiction. After a difficult, notorious divorce case Lawrence and Frieda were married in the summer of 1914. The publication of *Sons and Lovers* had brought Lawrence wider fame, but the outbreak of war trapped them in England for over five years. Still hard up, their finances received a jolt in 1915 when *The Rainbow* was seized by the police as 'obscene'. They were now dependent on Lawrence's small, if growing, royalties, grants from the Royal Literary fund and gifts or loans from friends and family. They settled for a year in Cornwall until ordered to leave by the wartime authorities, suspicious of Frieda's German origins. They then spent a year in a Derbyshire cottage, paid for by Lawrence's sister – Lawrence working prodigiously all the time at novels, poems, stories and journalism. He completed the first draft of *Women in Love* in only six weeks. In 1917 *Look! We Have Come Through!*, a collection of poems 'depicting' his first months with Frieda, was published.

Granted new passports in 1919, the Lawrences set off to travel – and did so for the rest of Lawrence's life – first to Italy, then on to Ceylon, Australia, Mexico and the United States. With the American publication of his work Lawrence's money problems were at last resolved (he began to repay loans) – without him ever losing the practical, parsimonious touch that kept the wolf from the door.

Lawrence, the cantankerous intellectual, was also an immensely practical man – they moved house constantly, but he scrubbed, decorated, sewed, knitted and made furniture to create a home wherever they stopped for any length of time. At the invitation of the American heiress Mabel Dodge Luhan the Lawrences settled in Taos, New Mexico, where Lawrence wrote *Kangaroo*, *The Plumed Serpent*, *St Mawr* and much more – but by 1925 his health had seriously deteriorated and he was diagnosed as having third-stage tuberculosis and given two years to live.

In November the same year Lawrence settled near Florence, in very poor health, probably impotent and wondering whether he could or should attempt another novel. Meanwhile Frieda began an affair with Angelo Ravagli.

A brief, final visit to England coincided with the prolonged miners' strike of 1926. Back in Italy Lawrence began his last novel, the first in several years to be set in his native Eastwood. Over the next two years he produced three different versions of *Lady Chatterley's Lover*, even preparing the 'expurgated' edition personally, while also writing a prodigious amount of poetry. The unexpurgated *Lady Chatterley's Lover* he published privately in Florence and sold by subscription. It made more money than any other novel in his lifetime – but in 1929 imported copies were seized by Scotland Yard, his paintings impounded in a London gallery and the typescript of his poems *Pansies* intercepted in the post. Whilst this latter action led to questions in the Commons about freedom and censorship, for Lawrence they were the last kicks from a country in which he felt abused and unappreciated.

He died on 2 March 1930 in Vence, France, aged forty-four.

Frieda returned to New Mexico, spent the rest of her life there, and in 1950 finally married Angelo Ravagli.

In 1932 Lawrence's *Last Poems* were published.

In 1959 Penguin books published the unexpurgated *Lady Chatterley's Lover* in England and, in one of the most famous trials in legal history, defeated the subsequent prosecution for obscenity, making Lawrence posthumously, probably, the most famous writer of the twentieth century.

JOHN LAWTON is the author of three novels – *Black Out*, *Old Flames* and *A Little White Death* (London: Weidenfeld & Nicolson). He has also edited H. G. Wells's *The Time Machine* and *When the Sleeper Wakes*, and D. H. Lawrence's *Short Stories* (London: Everyman).

Chronology of Lawrence's Life

Year	Age	Life
1885		D. H. Lawrence born, Eastwood, Nottinghamshire, 11 September
1886		
1891		
1892–1901	6–16	Beauvale Board School, followed by Nottingham High School
1893		
1895		
1899		
1900		
1901	15	Meets Jessie Chambers and her family
1902–6	16–21	Pupil-teacher at British School Eastwood, followed by course for pupil-teachers at Ilkeston
1903		Forms intellectual circle – 'The Pagans' – with Jessie Chambers and Louie Burrows, among others
1905		
1906–8	21–3	Attends Nottingham University College. Begins first novel, to be *The White Peacock*
1907	22	First publication, 'A Prelude', in the *Nottingham Guardian*

Chronology of his Times

Year	Artistic Events	Historical Events
1885		Death of General Gordon at Khartoum
1886	James, *The Bostonians*	Gladstone's Home Rule Bill for Ireland leads to Liberal defeat
1891	Hardy, *Tess of the D'Urbervilles*	
1892	Death of Tennyson and Whitman	
1893	Gissing, *The Odd Women*	Independent Labour Party formed
1895	Hardy, *Jude the Obscure*	
1899	Ellis, *Studies in the Psychology of Sex*	Boer War begins
1900	Conrad, *Lord Jim* Death of Nietzsche	British Labour Party founded Commonwealth of Australia proclaimed
1901		Death of Queen Victoria
1902	Conrad, *Heart of Darkness*	Boer War ends
1903		Women's Social and Political Union formed by Emmeline Pankhurst
1905	Shaw, *Major Barbara* Freud, *Three Essays on Sexuality*	Unrest in Russia Sinn Fein formed in Dublin
1906	Galsworthy, *The Man of Property*	Liberals win general election Women's Suffrage Movement becomes active
1907		

Year	Age	Life
1908	23	Teaching at Croydon
1909	24	Meets Ford Madox Ford (Hueffer) who publishes some of his early works in *English Review*. Writes 'Odour of Chrysanthemums'
1910	25	Engagement to Louie Burrows. Death of Lydia Lawrence (mother). Begins writing *The Trespasser, Sons and Lovers*
1911	25	Meets Edward Garnett. *The White Peacock* published. Seriously ill with pneumonia
1912	26	Abandons teaching career and leaves Croydon. Breaks engagement to Louie Burrows. Meets Frieda Weekley and travels to Germany and Italy with her. *The Trespasser* published
1913	27	Returns to England with Frieda. Breaks relationship with Jessie Chambers. *Love Poems, Sons and Lovers* published. Returns to Italy and begins writing *The Sisters* (later *The Rainbow*)
1914	28	Returns to England. Marries Frieda Weekley, 13 July. *The Widowing of Mrs Holroyd, The Prussian Officer* published
1915	29	Meets Aldous Huxley. Plans a series of lectures with Bertrand Russell. Living in Sussex and London. Writes 'Study of Thomas Hardy'. *The Rainbow* published and almost immediately suppressed
1916	30	Living in Cornwall. Undergoes two medical examinations and pronounced unfit for military service. *Women in Love* completed. *Twilight in Italy, Amores* published
1917	31	The Lawrences are suspected of being spies and expelled from Cornwall. Living in Berkshire and London. *Look! We Have Come Through!* published. Begins writing *Aaron's Rod*

Year	Artistic Events	Historical Events
1908	Bennett, *The Old Wives Tale*	
1909	Death of Swinburne	Old Age pension introduced
1910	Forster, *Howard's End*	Death of Edward VII Accession of George V
1911	Conrad, *Under Western Eyes* Brooke, *Poems*	Suffrage riots in London National Insurance introduced
1912	Georgian Poetry anthologies begin	Parliament rejects Women's Franchise Bill
1913		House of Commons passes Irish Home Rule Bill Suffragette demonstrations in London. 'Cat and Mouse' Act passed
1914	Joyce, *Dubliners* First anthology of *Imagist Poetry*	Britain declares war on Germany, 4 August
1915	Ford, *The Good Soldier* Woolf, *The Voyage Out*	Gallipoli landings
1916	H. D., *Sea Garden* Joyce, *Portrait of the Artist as a Young Man* Shaw, *Pygmalion* Death of Henry James	Lloyd George becomes prime minister Conscription introduced Easter Rising, Dublin Battle of the Somme
1917	Eliot, *Prufrock and Other Observations* Shaw, *Heartbreak House*	Russian Revolution US declares war on Germany Passchendaele

Year	Age	Life
1918	32	Living in Derbyshire. Lawrence undergoes third medical examination. *New Poems* published. Writes *The Fox*
1919	33	Lawrences leave England to live in Italy. *Bay: A book of Poems* published
1920	34	Living in Sicily. *The Lost Girl* published; *Women in Love* published in New York
1921	35	Living in Sardinia, Germany and Capri. Writes 'The Captain's Doll', 'The Ladybird'. *Movements in European History, Psychoanalysis and the Unconscious* and *Sea and Sardinia* published
1922	36	Visits Ceylon, Australia, California and New Mexico, settling in Lobo, near Taos. Begins writing *Kangaroo*. *Aaron's Rod, Fantasia of the Unconscious* and *England my England* published
1923	37	Visits Mexico. Returns briefly to London. Arthur Lawrence (father) dies. Begins writing *The Plumed Serpent*. *The Ladybird, Studies in Classic American Literature, Kangaroo* and *Birds, Beasts and Flowers* published
1924	38	Living in New Mexico and Mexico. Begins writing *St Mawr, The Woman who Rode Away*. *The Boy in the Bush* published
1925	39	Doctor tells Frieda that Lawrence is dying of tuberculosis. They settle in Florence in September. *St Mawr* and *Reflections on the Death of a Porcupine* published
1926	40	Brief visit to London. Return to Florence. Starts writing *Lady Chatterley's Lover* and *The Virgin and the Gipsy*. *The Plumed Serpent* and *David* published
1927	41	Visits Etruria. Writing *The Escaped Cock, Etruscan Places*. *Mornings in Mexico* published

Year	Artistic Events	Historical Events
1918	Brooke, Collected Poems	First World War ends, 11 November. Women over thirty granted the vote
1919	Hardy, Collected Poems Freud, Beyond the Pleasure Principle	Treaty of Versailles Nancy Astor, first woman MP
1920	Thomas, Collected Poems	League of Nations formed Prohibition in United States
1921	H. D., Hymen	
1922	Eliot, The Waste Land Joyce, Ulysses Sitwell, Facade Woolf, Jacob's Room	Proclamation of Irish Free State Mussolini's rise to power in Italy
1923	Yeats awarded Nobel Prize	Establishment of USSR British Matrimonial Causes Act awards equality to women in divorce proceedings German inflationary crisis
1924	Forster, A Passage to India Shaw, St Joan Death of Joseph Conrad	Ramsey Macdonald forms first Labour government Stalin becomes Soviet dictator
1925	Shaw awarded Nobel Prize Woolf, Mrs Dalloway Yeats, A Vision	Hitler, Mein Kampf
1926	T. E. Lawrence, Seven Pillars of Wisdom	General Strike BBC founded
1927	Woolf, To the Lighthouse Forster, Aspects of the Novel	Lindbergh makes first solo crossing of the Atlantic

Year	Age	Life
1928	42	Living in Switzerland; visits the South of France. Writing 'The Man who Died'. *The Woman who Rode Away, Lady Chatterley's Lover* and *Collected Poems* published
1929	43	Visits France, Majorca and Germany. Lawrence's work is seized in a raid on an exhibition of his paintings. Writing 'A Propos of Lady Chatterley's Lover', *Apocalypse, Last Poems. Paintings of D. H. Lawrence* and *Pansies* published
1930	44	D. H. Lawrence dies, Vence, south of France, 2 March. *The Virgin and the Gipsy* published
1931		*Apocalypse* published
1932		*Etruscan Places, Letters* (ed. Huxley) and *Last Poems* published
1933		'The Ship of Death' published
1934		
1935		Lawrence's ashes are taken to Taos where a shrine has been prepared for them

Year	Artistic Events	Historical Events
1928	Death of Thomas Hardy Radclyffe Hall, *The Well of Loneliness* Shaw, *The Intellectual Woman's Guide to Socialism and Capitalism* Woolf, *Orlando* Yeats, *The Tower*	Women over the age of twenty-one enfranchised
1929	Woolf, *A Room of One's Own* Yeats, *The Winding Stair*	Wall Street Crash
1930		Nazi party win seats in German elections
1931	Woolf, *The Waves* Death of Bennett	Ramsay Macdonald forms National Government
1932	Huxley, *Brave New World* Leavis, *New Bearings in English Poetry*	Hunger marches Mosley founds British Union of Fascists
1933		Hitler becomes Chancellor of Germany
1934	Waugh, *A Handful of Dust*	Hitler becomes Fuhrer. Third Reich proclaimed in Germany
1935	Eliot, *Murder in the Cathedral* Isherwood, *Mr Norris Changes Trains*	Italy invades Abyssinia Germany rearms

Introduction

There is one precondition for reading D. H. Lawrence – you cannot afford to mind being preached at. He is messianic. Like it or lump it.

This does not make Lawrence a difficult poet – quite the opposite. He is non-aligned, not only with the more lyrical Neo-Georgians of the years just before the war (although he shared the same anthology pages with them) but also non-aligned with the more complex Imagists who followed. His sense of mission notwithstanding, his verse is on the whole very accessible. The distinction I would accord his poetry is to say that as a novelist he peaked early, as a story-writer he was hit-and-miss, but as a poet, a few ups and downs allowed for, he grew throughout his short writing life.

Lawrence was never unsure of his subject. He knew what he wanted to write 'about' from the start: the relationship between men and women. If this sounds like a truism, then let me point out that the desire to write – to 'be a writer' if you like – often exists without the subject matter or the style that would turn fantasy into writing. Sure of his subject, but in much of his early verse uncertain of his styles – and I do mean the plural – often trying and failing to make poetry out of the material of his everyday life. For the first collected edition of his poems in 1928 Lawrence regrouped his work into Rhyming and Unrhyming poems – the former being four books of poetry (*Love Poems, Amores, New Poems, Bay*). That he regrouped them so I see as a way of hiving off much of his early work, a tad short of labelling it juvenilia. He also took the opportunity to revise many of them. In these early poems Lawrence is already working with the themes and ideas that will run through his fiction – indeed there seems to be no difference at all between his verse and his fiction in terms of subject, only of impulse, but his verse strikes me as often hampered by fractured rhyme-schemes and by an overblown vocabulary that, stuck with such subjects as his teaching days in Croydon, jar madly. Much of the early verse is gawky – long-legged and spotty. Ironically, the heightened vocabulary of poetry (the private, the intimate language made public) works better in his prose, as though the glossary of Lawrentian terms were more acceptable as dialogue or when thinned out by the scale of narrative and character – at which point 'poetic' and 'prosaic' cease to be wholly useful as descriptive terms.

My choice in the early poetry has been the simpler poems (often harking back to the work of Hardy or Wordsworth and even further to Blake) such as 'Cherry Robbers' or 'Endless Anxiety' – or for the dialect poems such as 'The Collier's Wife'. If 'The Collier's Wife' reads like one of his short stories, then 'Discipline' should be familiar to anyone who has read *The Rainbow*, and the event described in 'Cherry Robbers' can be found in prose in Chapter 11 of *Sons and Lovers*.

Whilst most of the early verse was written before 1913 (*Bay* dates from 1917) their publication in book form was staggered – *New Poems* and *Bay* did not appear until 1919. In the 'middle' or thereabouts of Rhyming Poems, came *Look! We Have Come Through!* The title alone speaks of self-liberation, and that Lawrence chose this collection to head the order of Unrhyming Poems says what he thinks of it. He has divided his work in terms not only of theme but also in terms of its worth. He has set *Look! We Have Come Through!* apart. It is, to the author, the volume that turned him around as a poet. It isn't anything as simple as the abandonment of rhyme for free verse – as T. S. Eliot put it, 'no verse is ever free',[1] and many of the poems rhyme regardless of the new heading. I suspect Lawrence's self-assessment was right when he wrote that the death of his mother was 'the long haunting of death in life' which runs through to *Bay* (see 'Sorrow', 'A Window', 'Endless Anxiety'), and that the parallel process – love, Frieda, elopement, marriage – that begins with *Look! We Have Come Through!* became his liberation – the right subject in the right form. The voice is uniquely Lawrence's.

'Snap-Dragon' – easily one of his best early poems and a structure so heavy with sexual symbolism that one of its achievements is that it stays up without caving in – is by 1912, for want of a better word, 'dated'. There is probably no more than a matter of months between 'Snap-Dragon' and the first poems of the new collection, but the intense sexual frustration of the poem is eclipsed by the consummation with Frieda. She was not his first lover, but the exploitations, the frustrations of snatched weekends are over. Two years after he surrendered it physically Lawrence is, at last, free from the tawny hand of his own long-redundant virginity –

metaphorically. He no longer has to imagine sex (he had sketched his fiancée Louie Burrows in the nude not from life but purely from imagination) or to pretend to sex, merely to remember it – but then memory itself is another form of imagining.

I've chosen only half a dozen or so from *Look! We Have Come Through!* The poems in this volume are in a double-bind. They are Lawrence's near-daily chronicle of his non-marriage, the prolonged 'honeymoon' of his travels with Frieda – itinerant adulterers on the Continent in the last months of the long peace – in all their joy and misery. Many of them are place-named at the end, much as one would date or place a diary entry. Bert and Frieda do indeed 'come through' – the eventual triumphant note of the poems is unmistakable – but I've always had a sneaking sympathy with Bertrand Russell's reaction to their publication. 'I'm glad they've come through, but do I have to look?' Not because Lawrence offers an unacceptable frankness – but because he does not. He is stretching both style and subject – they are bold poems for their time (the publisher insisted on two poems being dropped), but not bold enough, and the result seems to be a coyness that requires a key. Revising one of the early dialect poems Lawrence put 'cunt'[2] into print in 1928. He made no such change to *Look! We Have Come Through!* – yet what the volume lacks (and much of his work lacked until he wrote *Lady Chatterley's Lover*) is a medium that will let him use that, or any other of the 'scapegoat' words – words I do not think he regarded as exclusively dialect – just when the subject demands that he does. In the best of the poems, as the poet Horace Gregory remarked, 'there is a Renoir quality painted over the surface . . . but what lies under has a different texture . . . [a] sudden depth'. And, by and large, it's poems like this that I've plumped for – 'Gloire de Dijon', 'Roses on the Breakfast Table' – in preference to Lawrence's exultant manifestos.

If what I've written so far sounds negative, I'll say straightaway that it is with the next volume, *Birds, Beasts and Flowers* (1923), that I think Lawrence comes into his own as a poet. It is a strikingly original collection, and includes some of Lawrence's best-known poems.

I've never been able to think of *Birds, Beasts and Flowers* as simple anthropomorphism. Lawrence's subjects are symbolic – and, inevitably, from the symbol hangs a lesson – but with symbols he's aiming at something other than investing the inanimate with the animate, or the animate with the human – he's aiming, by his own definition, lower than that. Lawrence is looking at the non-human element, the 'carbon', as he called it, beneath mankind – as he put it in a letter to his friend Catherine Carswell 'we must have the courage to cast off the old symbols'. 'Cypresses' is a good example. A symbol of his own making. The tree stands not for any human, any individual, or any human feeling – it stands for an entire civilisation, and for the 'carbon, non-human element', as Lawrence insisted, beneath that civilisation.

At the other extreme, for all that it is highly symbolic in most cultures, is there any need to look for a symbolic value in 'Snake'? Is it anything more or less than the meeting of man and beast – the snake being snakeish and the man being mannish (and regretting it) – is there a better poem in Lawrence's work? It is a work, like so much of *Birds, Beasts and Flowers*, of remarkable empathy – as the poet D. J. Enright puts it 'like Adam among the animals' – or, as Lawrence might have put it himself, alive to the otherness of the other.

In 1926, as he resettled in Italy, Lawrence mused, queried and several times asserted that he was through with the novel. ('Why write books for the swine, unless one absolutely must!' 'I don't feel much like writing a book of any sort.' 'I feel I'll never write another novel.') He'd finished *The Plumed Serpent* (not one of his best) and over the next year wrote the three versions of *Lady Chatterley's Lover*. It's fair to say that he was living on borrowed time and knew it. He was probably impotent by now, although I'm sure the neologism might well be to say that he was 'post-sexual'. There are a few short stories after this point, one of his best travel books, *Etruscan Places*, and a number of paintings – yet there is a vast amount of poetry. Nearly half of Lawrence's verse is to be found in *Pansies* (1929) and *Last Poems* (1932). Poetry at this point in his working life was his working life. Post-fiction, and, yes, post-sex, poetry became his form. And what a curious form it is. The title is a play on *Pensées*: Thoughts. If I say that *Pansies* is a difficult collection, I don't mean that the poems are inherently complex. I mean 'what are they?'

For many critics they will be the biggest of the 'downs' in the ups and downs I spoke of earlier. Horace Gregory, the first of Lawrence's friends to write a serious study of his work, rather than a memoir of the man, sums them up as 'doggerel', 'pus and venom', 'a species of journalism', devoid of 'wit', full of 'petty, malicious anger' and, worse still, 'dull reading'. What Lawrence set out are clusters of meditations – unrhyming poems – he would not admit to 'prose poems', as he makes clear in his introduction – with the occasional foray into verse more often than not indicating that the tongue is firmly in the cheek or the knives out – eddying around such subjects as money, ego, class, sex, patriotism and, above all else, England – sometimes in twos and threes, sometimes as many as eight or nine to a cluster. As Gregory implies, they are the work of a man in isolation, cut off from the English-speaking countries by choice and ill-health, who seems to be provoked to rage by his one point of contact – newspapers. A prismatic vision of his native land. The risk in over-emphasising this is to make Lawrence into Disgruntled of Tunbridge Wells. There's more to these poems than that – more, I will assert, than Gregory's early (1933) assessment will allow. They are hard, haranguing, abusive, radical, angry poems – I'm not entirely sure whether they're bitter too – but, above all, they seem to me to be the work of a man who, if not through with life, knows that it is through with him.

When Lawrence died in March 1930 some two hundred poems were found among his papers. They were published in 1932 as Last Poems, subdivided into *Last Poems* and *More Pansies*, with an introduction by Lawrence's friend and subsequent biographer Richard Aldington. They include the two poems which have since become the best known of Lawrence's poetry: 'The Ship of Death' and 'Bavarian Gentians'.

These last poems are different in tone and emphasis from *Pansies*. Less angry, darker. Lawrence is on the one hand back to attacking his old enemy the machine – and on the other waiting for, often welcoming, the prospect of death. There are echoes in this more peaceable Lawrence of *Birds, Beasts and Flowers* once more, of fruit that is ripe, then rotten, then seed – and with seed comes new life. Lawrence is embracing death, 'dipping into oblivion' as though it were the last big adventure – seeing in it the prospect of his own renewal. The last poem in this collection (and most others) is 'Phoenix' – the bird who, consumed by fire, rises from its own ashes. Lawrence adopted the phoenix as his personal symbol – his sketch of the bird figured on the title page of *Last Poems*. On the facing page was the last drawing he did – a crown of thorns. This is

Lawrence at the end – tormented by his own body, facing death, seeking rebirth.

JOHN LAWTON

References

1. Lawrence went to some trouble to describe what he meant by 'free verse' in an essay of 1919, 'Poetry of the Present':

   . . . free verse has its own nature . . . neither star nor pearl, but instantaneous like plasm. It has no goal in either eternity. It has no finish. It has no satisfying stability, satisfying to those who like the immutable. None of this. It is the instant; the quick; the very jetting source of all will-be and has-been. The utterance is like a spasm, naked contact with all influences at once. It does not want to get anywhere. It just takes place.

   He then added 'all this should have come as a preface to *Look! We Have Come Through!*'

2. On obscenity Lawrence wrote:

   . . . I am mystified at this horror over a mere word, a plain simple word that stands for a plain simple thing. 'In the beginning was the Word and the Word was with God.' If that is true, then we are very far from the beginning. When did the Word 'fall'? When did the Word become unclean 'below the navel'? . . . If the Word is God – which in the sense of the human mind it is – then you can't suddenly say that all the words which belong below the navel are obscene. The word arse is as much God as the word face. It must be so, otherwise you cut your god off at the waist.

   (Introduction to *Pansies*, 1929)

D. H. Lawrence

Discord in Childhood

Outside the house an ash-tree hung its terrible whips,
And at night when the wind rose, the lash of the tree
Shrieked and slashed the wind, as a ship's
Weird rigging in a storm shrieks hideously.

Within the house two voices arose, a slender lash
Whistling she-delirious rage, and the dreadful sound
Of a male thong booming and bruising, until it had drowned
The other voice in a silence of blood, 'neath the noise of the
    ash.

Cherry Robbers

Under the long dark boughs, like jewels red
 In the hair of an Eastern girl
Hang strings of crimson cherries, as if had bled
 Blood-drops beneath each curl.

Under the glistening cherries, with folded wings
 Three dead birds lie:
Pale-breasted throstles and a blackbird, robberlings
 Stained with red dye.

Against the haystack a girl stands laughing at me,
 Cherries hung round her ears.
Offers me her scarlet fruit: I will see
 If she has any tears.

The Collier's Wife

Somebody's knockin' at th' door
    Mother, come down an' see!
– I's think it's nobbut a beggar;
    Say I'm busy.

It's not a beggar, mother; hark
    How 'ard 'e knocks!
– Eh, tha'rt a mard-arsed kid,
    'E'll gie thee socks!

Shout an' ax what 'e wants,
    I canna come down.
– 'E says, is it Arthur Holliday's?
    – Say Yes, tha clown.

'E says: Tell your mother as 'er mester's
    Got hurt i' th' pit—
What? Oh my Sirs, 'e never says that,
    That's not it!

Come out o' th' way an' let me see!
    Eh, there's no peace!
An' stop thy scraightin', childt,
    Do shut thy face!

'Your mester's 'ad a accident
    An' they ta'ein' 'im i' th' ambulance
Ter Nottingham.' – Eh dear o' me,
    If 'e's not a man for mischance!

Wheer's 'e hurt this time, lad?
    – I dunna know,
They on'y towd me it wor bad –
    It would be so!

Out o' my way, childt! dear o' me, wheer
    'Ave I put 'is clean stockin's an' shirt?
Goodness knows if they'll be able
    To take off 'is pit-dirt!

An' what a moan 'e'll make! there niver
    Was such a man for a fuss
If anything ailed 'im; at any rate
    I shan't 'ave 'im to nuss.

I do 'ope as it's not so very bad!
    Eh, what a shame it seems
As some should ha'e hardly a smite o' trouble
    An' others 'as reams!

It's a shame as 'e should be knocked about
    Like this, I'm sure it is!
'E's 'ad twenty accidents, if 'e's 'ad one;
    Owt bad, an' it's his!

There's one thing, we s'll 'ave a peaceful 'ouse f'r a
    bit,
    Thank heaven for a peaceful house!
An' there's compensation, sin' it's accident,
    An' club-money – I won't growse.

An' a fork an' a spoon 'e'll want – an' what else?
    I s'll never catch that train!
What a traipse it is, if a man gets hurt!
    I sh'd think 'e'll get right again.

Violets

Sister, tha knows while we was on th' planks
    Aside o' t' grave, an' th' coffin set
Oh th' yaller clay, wi' th' white flowers top of it
    Waitin' ter be buried out o' th' wet?

An't' parson makin' haste, an' a' t' black
    Huddlin' up i' t' rain,
Did t' 'appen ter notice a bit of a lass way back
    Hoverin', lookin' poor an' plain?

      – How should I be lookin' round!
        An' me standin' there on th' plank,
        An' our Ted's coffin set on th' ground,
        Waitin' to be sank!

      I'd as much as I could do, to think
        Of 'im bein' gone
      That young, an' a' the fault of drink
        An' carryin's on! –

Let that be; 'appen it worna th' drink, neither,
Nor th' carryin' on as killed 'im.
                – No, 'appen not,
My sirs! But I say 'twas! For a blither
Lad never stepped, till 'e got in with your lot. –

All right, all right, it's my fault! But let
Me tell about that lass. When you'd all gone
Ah stopped behind on t' pad, i' t' pourin' wet
An' watched what 'er 'ad on.

Tha should ha' seed 'er slive up when yer'd gone!
Tha should ha' seed 'er kneel an' look in
At th' sloppy grave! an' 'er little neck shone
That white, an' 'er cried that much, I'd like to begin

Scraightin' mysen as well. 'Er undid 'er black
Jacket at th' bosom, an' took out
Over a double 'andful o' violets, a' in a pack
An' white an' blue in a ravel, like a clout.

An' warm, for th' smell come waftin' to me. 'Er put 'er face
Right in 'em, an' scraighted a bit again,
Then after a bit 'er dropped 'em down that place,
An' I come away, acause o' th' teemin' rain.

But I thowt ter mysen, as that wor th' only bit
O' warmth as 'e got down theer; th' rest wor stone cold.
From that bit of a wench's bosom; 'e'd be glad of it,
Gladder nor of thy lilies, if tha maun be told.

Corot*

The trees rise taller and taller, lifted
On a subtle rush of cool grey flame
That issuing out of the east has sifted
    The spirit from each leaf's frame.

For the trailing, leisurely rapture of life
Drifts dimly forward, easily hidden
By bright leaves uttered aloud; and strife
    Of shapes by a hard wind ridden,

The grey, plasm-limpid, pellucid advance
Of the luminous purpose of Life shines out
Where lofty trees athwart-stream chance
    To shake flakes of its shadow about.

The subtle, steady rush of the whole
Grey foam-mist of advancing Time
As it silently sweeps to its somewhere, its goal,
    Is seen in the gossamer's rime.

Is heard in the windless whisper of leaves,
In the silent labours of men in the field,
In the downward-dropping of flimsy sheaves
    Of cloud the rain-skies yield.

In the tapping haste of a fallen leaf,
In the flapping of red-roof smoke, and the small
Footstepping tap of men beneath
    Dim trees so huge and tall.

For what can all sharp-rimmed substance but catch
In a backward ripple, the wave-length, reveal
For a moment the mighty direction, snatch
    A spark beneath the wheel!

Since Life sweeps whirling, dim and vast,
Creating the channelled vein of man
And leaf for its passage; a shadow cast
    And gone before we can scan.

Ah listen, for silence is not lonely!
Imitate the magnificent trees
That speak no word of their rapture, but only
    Breathe largely the luminous breeze.

Morning Work

A gang of labourers on the piled wet timber
That shines blood-red beside the railway siding
Seem to be making out of the blue of the morning
Something faery and fine, the shuttles sliding,

The red-gold spools of their hands and their faces swinging
Hither and thither across the high crystalline frame
Of day: trolls at the cave of ringing cerulean mining
And laughing with labour, living their work like a game.

Discipline

It is stormy, and raindrops cling like silver bees to the panes,
The thin sycamore in the playground is swinging with flattened
    leaves;
The heads of the boys move dimly through a yellow gloom that
    stains
The class; over them all the dark net of my discipline weaves.

It is no good, dear, gentleness and forbearance; I endured too
    long.
I have pushed my hands in the dark soil, under the flower of my
    soul
And the gentle leaves, and have felt where the roots are strong
Fixed in the darkness, grappling for the deep soil's crowded
    control.

And there in the dark, my darling, where the roots are entangled
    and fight
Each one for its hold on the concrete darkness, I know that there
In the night where we first have being, before we rise on the
    light,
We are not lovers, my darling, we fight and we do not spare.

And in the original dark the roots cannot keep, cannot know
Any communion whatever, but they bind themselves on to the
    dark,
And drawing the darkness together, crush from it a twilight, a
    slow
Dim self that rises slowly to leaves and the flower's gay spark.

I came to the boys with love, dear, and only they turned on me;
With gentleness came I, with my heart 'twixt my hands like a
    bowl,
Like a loving-cup, like a grail, but they split it triumphantly
And tried to break the vessel, and violate my soul.

And perhaps they were right, for the young are busy deep down
    at the roots,

And love would only weaken their under-earth grip, make
shallow
Their hold on reality, enfeeble their rising shoots
With too much tincture of me, instead of the dark's deep fallow.

I thought that love would do all things, but now I know I am
wrong.
There are depths below depths, my darling, where love does not
belong.
Where the fight that is fight for being is fought throughout the
long
Young years, and the old must not win, not even if they love and
are strong.

I must not win their souls, no never, I only must win
The brief material control of the hour, leave them free of me.
Learn they must to obey, for all harmony is discipline,
And only in harmony with others the single soul can be free.

Let them live, the boys, and learn not to trespass; I had to learn
Not to trespass on them with love, they must learn not to
trespass in the young
Cruel self; the fight is not for existence, the fight is to burn
At last into blossom of being, each one his own flower outflung.

They are here to learn but one lesson, that they shall not thwart
each other
Nor be thwarted, in life's slow struggle to unfold the flower of the
self.
They draw their sap from the Godhead, not from me, but they
must not smother
The sun from their neighbour either, nor be smothered in turn by
pelf.

I will teach them the beginning of the lesson at the roots, and
then no more.
I throw from out of the darkness myself like a flower into sight
Of the day, but it's nothing to do with the boys, so let them ignore
What's beyond them, and fight with me in discipline's little fight.

But whoever would pluck apart my flowering will burn their
hands,
For flowers are tender folk, and roots can only hide.
But sometimes the opening petals are fire, and the scarlet brands

Of the blossom are roses to look at, but flames when they're tried.

But now I am trodden to earth, and my fires are low;
Now I am broken down like a plant in winter, and all
Myself but a knowledge of roots, of roots in the dark, that throw
A net on the undersoil, that lies passive, and quickened with gall.

Yet wait awhile, for henceforth I will love when a blossom calls
To my blossom in perfume and seed-dust, and only then; I will
give
My love where it is wanted. Yet wait awhile! My fall
Is complete for the moment, yet wait, and you'll see that my
flower will live.

Endless Anxiety

The hoar-frost crumbles in the sun,
    The crisping steam of a train
Melts in the air, while two black birds
    Sweep past the window again.

Along the vacant road a red
    Telegram-bicycle approaches; I wait
In a thaw of anxiety, for the boy
    To leap down at our gate.

He has passed us by; but is it
    Relief that starts in my breast?
Or a deeper bruise of knowing that still
    She has no rest.

At the Window

The pine-trees bend to listen to the autumn wind as it mutters
Something which sets the black poplars ashake with hysterical
    laughter;
As slowly the house of day is closing its eastern shutters.

Farther down the valley the clustered tombstones recede,
Winding about their dimness the mist's grey cerements, after
The street-lamps in the twilight have suddenly started to bleed.

The leaves fly over the window, and utter a word as they pass
To the face that gazes outwards, watching for night to waft a
Meaning or a message over the window glass.

Sorrow

Why does the thin grey strand
Floating up from the forgotten
Cigarette between my fingers,
Why does it trouble me?

Ah, you will understand;
When I carried my mother downstairs,
A few times only, at the beginning
Of her soft-foot malady,

I should find, for a reprimand
To my gaiety, a few long grey hairs
On the breast of my coat; and one by one
I watched them float up the dark chimney.

Snap-Dragon

She bade me follow to her garden, where
The mellow sunlight stood as in a cup
Between the old grey walls; I did not dare
To raise my face, I did not dare look up,
Lest her bright eyes like sparrows should fly in
My windows of discovery, and shrill 'Sin!'

So with a downcast mien and laughing voice
I followed, followed the swing of her white dress
That rocked in a lilt along; I watched the poise
Of her feet as they flew for a space, then paused to press
The grass deep down with the royal burden of her;
And gladly I'd offered my breast to the tread of her.

'I like to see,' she said, and she crouched her down,
She sunk into my sight like a settling bird;
And her bosom couched in the confines of her gown
Like heavy birds at rest there, softly stirred
By her measured breaths: 'I like to see,' said she,
'The snap-dragon put out his tongue at me.'

She laughed, she reached her hand out to the flower,
Closing its crimson throat. My own throat in her power
Strangled, my heart swelled up so full
As if it would burst its wine-skin in my throat,
Choke me in my own crimson. I watched her pull
The gorge of the gaping flower, till the blood did float

Over my eyes, and I was blind –
Her large brown hand stretched over
The windows of my mind;
And there in the dark I did discover
Things I was out to find:

My Grail, a brown bowl twined
With swollen veins that met in the wrist,
Under whose brown the amethyst
I longed to taste! I longed to turn
My heart's red measure in her cup;
I longed to feel my hot blood burn
With the amethyst in her cup.

Then suddenly she looked up,
And I was blind in a tawny-gold day,
Till she took her eyes away.

So she came down from above
And emptied my heart of love.
So I held my heart aloft
To the cuckoo that hung like a dove,
And she settled soft.

It seemed that I and the morning world
Were pressed cup-shape to take this reiver
Bird who was weary to have furled
Her wings in us,
As we were weary to receive her.

> *This bird, this rich,*
> *Sumptuous central grain;*
> *This mutable witch,*
> *This one refrain,*
> *This laugh in the fight,*
> *This clot of night,*
> *This field of delight.*

She spoke, and I closed my eyes
To shut hallucinations out.
I echoed with surprise
Hearing my mere lips shout
The answer they did devise.

> Again I saw a brown bird hover
> Over the flowers at my feet;

I felt a brown bird hover
Over my heart, and sweet
Its shadow lay on my heart.
I thought I saw on the clover
A brown bee pulling apart
The closed flesh of the clover
And burrowing in its heart.

She moved her hand, and again
I felt the brown bird cover
My heart; and then
The bird came down on my heart,
As on a nest the rover
Cuckoo comes, and shoves over
The brim each careful part
Of love, takes possession, and settles her down,
With her wings and her feathers to drown
The nest in a heat of love.

She turned her flushed face to me for the glint
Of a moment. – 'See,' she laughed, 'if you also
Can make them yawn!' – I put my hand to the dint
In the flower's throat, and the flower gaped wide with woe.
She watched, she went of a sudden intensely still,
She watched my hand, to see what it would fulfil.

I pressed the wretched, throttled flower between
My fingers, till its head lay back, its fangs
Poised at her. Like a weapon my hand was white and keen,
And I held the choked flower-serpent in its pangs
Of mordant anguish, till she ceased to laugh,
Until her pride's flag, smitten, cleaved down to the staff.

She hid her face, she murmured between her lips
The low word 'Don't!' – I let the flower fall,
But held my hand afloat towards the slips
Of blossom she fingered, and my fingers all
Put forth to her: she did not move, nor I,
For my hand like a snake watched hers, that could not fly.

Then I laughed in the dark of my heart, I did exult
Like a sudden chuckling of music. I bade her eyes
Meet mine, I opened her helpless eyes to consult
Their fear, their shame, their joy that underlies
Defeat in such a battle. In the dark of her eyes
My heart was fierce to make her laughter rise.

Till her dark deeps shook with convulsive thrills, and the dark
Of her spirit wavered like water thrilled with light;
And my heart leaped up in longing to plunge its stark
Fervour within the pool of her twilight,
Within her spacious soul, to find delight.

And I do not care, though the large hands of revenge
Shall get my throat at last, shall get it soon,
If the joy that they are lifted to avenge
Have risen red on my night as a harvest moon,
Which even death can only put out for me;
And death, I know, is better than not-to-be.

Blueness

Out of the darkness, fretted sometimes in its sleeping,
Jets of sparks in fountains of blue come leaping
To sight, revealing a secret, numberless secrets keeping.

Sometimes the darkness trapped within a wheel
Runs into speed like a dream, the blue of the steel
Showing the rocking darkness now a-reel.

And out of the invisible, streams of bright blue drops
Rain from the showery heavens, and bright blue crops
Of flowers surge from below to their ladder-tops.

And all the manifold blue, amazing eyes,
The rainbow arching over in the skies,
New sparks of wonder opening in surprise:

All these pure things come foam and spray of the sea
Of Darkness abundant, which shaken mysteriously
Breaks into dazzle of living, as dolphins leap from the sea
Of midnight and shake it to fire, till the flame of the shadow
    we see.

Piano

Softly, in the dusk, a woman is singing to me;
Taking me back down the vista of years, till I see
A child sitting under the piano, in the boom of the tingling
    strings
And pressing the small, poised feet of a mother who smiles as she
    sings.

In spite of myself, the insidious mastery of song
Betrays me back, till the heart of me weeps to belong
To the old Sunday evenings at home, with winter outside
And hymns in the cosy parlour, the tinkling piano our guide.

So now it is vain for the singer to burst into clamour
With the great black piano appassionato. The glamour
Of childish days is upon me, my manhood is cast
Down in the flood of remembrance, I weep like a child for the
    past.

Rondeau of a Conscientious Objector

The hours have tumbled their leaden, monotonous sands
And piled them up in a dull grey heap in the west.
I carry my patience sullenly through the waste lands;
To-morrow will pour them all back, the dull hours I detest.

I force my cart through the sodden filth that is pressed
Into ooze, and the sombre dirt spouts up at my hands
As I make my way in twilight now to rest.
The hours have tumbled their leaden, monotonous sands.

A twisted thorn-tree still in the evening stands
Defending the memory of leaves and the happy round nest.
But mud has flooded the homes of these weary lands
And piled them up in a dull grey heap in the west.

All day has the clank of iron on iron distressed
The nerve-bare place. Now a little silence expands
And a gasp of relief. But the soul is still compressed;
I carry my patience sullenly through the waste lands.

The hours have ceased to fall, and a star commands
Shadows to cover our stricken manhood, and blest
Sleep to make us forget: but he understands:
To-morrow will pour them all back, the dull hours I detest.

Humiliation

I have been so innerly proud, and so long alone,
Do not leave me, or I shall break.
Do not leave me.

What should I do if you were gone again
So soon?
What should I look for?
Where should I go?
What should I be, I myself,
'I'?
What would it mean, this
I?

Do not leave me.

What should I think of death?
If I died, it would not be you:
It would be simply the same
Lack of you.
The same want, life or death,
Unfulfilment,
The same insanity of space,
You not there for me.

Think, I daren't die
For fear of the lack in death.
And I daren't live.

Unless there were a morphine or a drug.

I would bear the pain.
But always, strong, unremitting
It would make me not me.
The thing with my body that would go on living

Would not be me.
Neither life nor death could help.

Think, I couldn't look towards death
Nor towards the future:
Only not look.
Only myself
Stand still and bind and blind myself.

God, that I have no choice!
That my own fulfilment is up against me
Timelessly!
The burden of self-accomplishment!
The charge of fulfilment!
And God, that she is *necessary*!
Necessary, and I have no choice!

Do not leave me.

A Young Wife

The pain of loving you
Is almost more than I can bear.

I walk in fear of you.
The darkness starts up where
You stand, and the night comes through
Your eyes when you look at me.

Ah never before did I see
The shadows that live in the sun!

Now every tall glad tree
Turns round its back to the sun
And looks down on the ground, to see
The shadow it used to shun.

At the foot of each glowing thing
A night lies looking up.

Oh, and I want to sing
And dance, but I can't lift up
My eyes from the shadows: dark
They lie spilt round the cup.

What is it? – Hark
The faint fine seethe in the air!

Like the seething sound in a shell!
It is death still seething where
The wild-flower shakes its bell
And the skylark twinkles blue –

The pain of loving you
Is almost more than I can bear.

Green

The dawn was apple-green,
　The sky was green wine held up in the sun,
The moon was a golden petal between.

She opened her eyes, and green
　They shone, clear like flowers undone
For the first time, now for the first time seen.
Icking.

Gloire de Dijon

When she rises in the morning
I linger to watch her;
She spreads the bath-cloth underneath the window
And the sunbeams catch her
Glistening white on the shoulders,
While down her sides the mellow
Golden shadow glows as
She stoops to the sponge, and her swung breasts
Sway like full-blown yellow
Gloire de Dijon roses.

She drips herself with water, and her shoulders
Glisten as silver, they crumple up
Like wet and falling roses, and I listen
For the sluicing of their rain-dishevelled petals.
In the window full of sunlight
Concentrates her golden shadow
Fold on fold, until it glows as
Mellow as the glory roses.

Icking.

Roses on the Breakfast Table

Just a few of the roses we gathered from the Isar
Are fallen, and their mauve-red petals on the cloth
Float like boats on a river, while other
Roses are ready to fall, reluctant and loth.

She laughs at me across the table, saying
I am beautiful. I look at the rumpled young roses
And suddenly realize, in them as in me,
How lovely is the self this day discloses.

A Doe at Evening

As I went through the marshes
a doe sprang out of the corn
and flashed up the hillside
leaving her fawn.

On the sky-line
she moved round to watch,
she pricked a fine black blotch
on the sky.

I looked at her
and felt her watching;
I became a strange being.
Still, I had my right to be there with her.

Her nimble shadow trotting
along the sky-line, she
put back her fine, level-balanced head.
And I knew her.

Ah yes, being male, is not my head hard-balanced, antlered?
Are not my haunches light?
Has she not fled on the same wind with me?
Does not my fear cover her fear?

                                        Irschenhausen

Giorno dei Morti*

Along the avenue of cypresses,
All in their scarlet cloaks and surplices
Of linen, go the chanting choristers,
The priests in gold and black, the villagers. . . .

And all along the path to the cemetery
The round dark heads of men crowd silently,
And black-scarved faces of womenfolk, wistfully
Watch at the banner of death, and the mystery.

And at the foot of a grave a father stands
With sunken head; and forgotten, folded hands;
And at the foot of a grave a mother kneels
With pale shut face, nor either hears nor feels

The coming of the chanting choristers
Between the avenue of cypresses,
The silence of the many villagers,
The candle-flames beside the surplices.

Medlars and Sorb-Apples

I love you, rotten,
Delicious rottenness.

I love to suck you out from your skins
So brown and soft and coming suave,
So morbid, as the Italians say.

What a rare, powerful, reminiscent flavour
Comes out of your falling through the stages of decay:
Stream within stream.

Something of the same flavour as Syracusan muscat wine
Or vulgar Marsala.

Though even the word Marsala will smack of preciosity
Soon in the pussyfoot West.

What is it?
What is it, in the grape turning raisin,
In the medlar, in the sorb-apple,
Wineskins of brown morbidity,
Autumnal excrementa;
What is it that reminds us of white gods?

Gods nude as blanched nut-kernels,
Strangely, half-sinisterly flesh-fragrant
As if with sweat,
And drenched with mystery.

Sorb-apples, medlars with dead crowns.
I say, wonderful are the hellish experiences,
Orphic, delicate
Dionysos of the Underworld.

A kiss, and a spasm of farewell, a moment's orgasm of rupture,

Then along the damp road alone, till the next turning.
And there, a new partner, a new parting, a new unfusing into
      twain,
A new gasp of further isolation,
A new intoxication of loneliness, among decaying, frost-cold
      leaves.

Going down the strange lanes of hell, more and more intensely
      alone,
The fibres of the heart parting one after the other
And yet the soul continuing, naked-footed, ever more vividly
      embodied
Like a flame blown whiter and whiter
In a deeper and deeper darkness
Ever more exquisite, distilled in separation.

So, in the strange retorts of medlars and sorb-apples
The distilled essence of hell.
The exquisite odour of leave-taking.
          Jamque vale!
Orpheus, and the winding, leaf-clogged, silent lanes of hell.

Each soul departing with its own isolation,
Strangest of all strange companions,
And best.

Medlars, sorb-apples,
More than sweet
Flux of autumn
Sucked out of your empty bladders

And sipped down, perhaps, with a sip of Marsala
So that the rambling, sky-dropped grape can add its savour to
      yours,
Orphic farewell, and farewell, and farewell
And the *ego sum* of Dionysos
The *sono io* of perfect drunkenness
Intoxication of final loneliness.

                                        San Gervasio.

Figs

The proper way to eat a fig, in society,
Is to split it in four, holding it by the stump,
And open it, so that it is a glittering, rosy, moist, honied, heavy-
    petalled four-petalled flower.

Then you throw away the skin
Which is just like a four-sepalled calyx,
After you have taken off the blossom with your lips.

But the vulgar way
Is just to put your mouth to the crack, and take out the flesh in
    one bite.

Every fruit has its secret.

The fig is a very secretive fruit.
As you see it standing growing, you feel at once it is symbolic:
And it seems male.
But when you come to know it better, you agree with the
    Romans, it is female.

The Italians vulgarly say, it stands for the female part; the fig-
    fruit:
The fissure, the yoni,
The wonderful moist conductivity towards the centre.

Involved,
Inturned,
The flowering all inward and womb-fibrilled;
And but one orifice.

The fig, the horse-shoe, the squash-blossom.
Symbols.

There was a flower that flowered inward, womb-ward;
Now there is a fruit like a ripe womb.

It was always a secret.
That's how it should be, the female should always be secret.

There never was any standing aloft and unfolded on a bough
Like other flowers, in a revelation of petals;
Silver-pink peach, venetian green glass of medlars and sorb-
    apples,
Shallow wine-cups on short, bulging stems
Openly pledging heaven:
Here's to the thorn in flower! Here is to Utterance!
The brave, adventurous rosaceæ.

Folded upon itself, and secret unutterable,
And milky-sapped, sap that curdles milk and makes *ricotta*,
Sap that smells strange on your fingers, that even goats won't
    taste it;
Folded upon itself, enclosed like any Mohammedan woman,
Its nakedness all within-walls, its flowering forever unseen,
One small way of access only, and this close-curtained from the
    light;
Fig, fruit of the female mystery, covert and inward,
Mediterranean fruit, with your covert nakedness,
Where everything happens invisible, flowering and fertilisation,
    and fruiting
In the inwardness of your you, that eye will never see
Till it's finished, and you're over-ripe, and you burst to give up
    your ghost.

Till the drop of ripeness exudes,
And the year is over.

And then the fig has kept her secret long enough.
So it explodes, and you see through the fissure the scarlet.
And the fig is finished, the year is over.

That's how the fig dies, showing her crimson through the purple
    slit
Like a wound, the exposure of her secret, on the open day.
Like a prostitute, the bursten fig, making a show of her secret.

That's how women die too.

The year is fallen over-ripe,
The year of our women.
The year of our women is fallen over-ripe.
The secret is laid bare.
And rottenness soon sets in.
The year of our women is fallen over-ripe.

When Eve once knew *in her mind* that she was naked
She quickly sewed fig-leaves, and sewed the same for the man.
She'd been naked all her days before,
But till then, till that apple of knowledge, she hadn't had the fact
    on her mind.

She got the fact on her mind, and quickly sewed fig-leaves.
And women have been sewing ever since.
But now they stitch to adorn the bursten fig, not to cover it.
They have their nakedness more than ever on their mind,
And they won't let us forget it.

Now, the secret
Becomes an affirmation through moist, scarlet lips
That laugh at the Lord's indignation.

What then, good Lord! cry the women.
We have kept our secret long enough.
We are a ripe fig.
Let us burst into affirmation.

They forget, ripe figs won't keep.
Ripe figs won't keep.

Honey-white figs of the north, black figs with scarlet inside, of the
    south.
Ripe figs won't keep, won't keep in any clime.
What then, when women the world over have all bursten into
    self-assertion?
And bursten figs won't keep?

                                                            San Gervasio.

Cypresses

Tuscan cypresses,
What is it?

Folded in like a dark thought
For which the language is lost,
Tuscan cypresses, .
Is there a great secret?
Are our words no good?

The undeliverable secret,
Dead with a dead race and a dead speech, and yet
Darkly monumental in you,
Etruscan cypresses.

Ah, how I admire your fidelity,
Dark cypresses!

Is it the secret of the long-nosed Etruscans?
The long-nosed, sensitive-footed, subtly-smiling Etruscans,
Who made so little noise outside the cypress groves?

Among the sinuous, flame-tall cypresses
That swayed their length of darkness all around
Etruscan-dusky, wavering men of old Etruria:
Naked except for fanciful long shoes,
Going with insidious, half-smiling quietness
And some of Africa's imperturbable sang-froid
About a forgotten business.

What business, then?
Nay, tongues are dead, and words are hollow as hollow seed-
      pods,
Having shed their sound and finished all their echoing
Etruscan syllables,
That had the telling.

Yet more I see you darkly concentrate,
Tuscan cypresses,
On one old thought:
On one old slim imperishable thought, while you remain
Etruscan cypresses;
Dusky, slim marrow-thought of slender, flickering men of Etruria,
Whom Rome called vicious.

Vicious, dark cypresses:
Vicious, you supple, brooding, softly-swaying pillars of dark
    flame.
Monumental to a dead, dead race
Embowered in you!

Were they then vicious, the slender, tender-footed
Long-nosed men of Etruria?
Or was their way only evasive and different, dark, like cypress-
    trees in a wind?

They are dead, with all their vices,
And all that is left
Is the shadowy monomania of some cypresses
And tombs.

The smile, the subtle Etruscan smile still lurking
Within the tombs,
Etruscan cypresses.
He laughs longest who laughs last;
Nay, Leonardo only bungled the pure Etruscan smile.

What would I not give
To bring back the rare and orchid-like
Evil-yclept Etruscan?
For as to the evil
We have only Roman word for it,
Which I, being a little weary of Roman virtue,
Don't hang much weight on.

For oh, I know, in the dust where we have buried
The silenced races and all their abominations,

We have buried so much of the delicate magic of life.

There in the deeps
That churn the frankincense and ooze the myrrh,
Cypress shadowy,
Such an aroma of lost human life!

They say the fit survive,
But I invoke the spirits of the lost.
Those that have not survived, the darkly lost,
To bring their meaning back into life again,
Which they have taken away
And wrapt inviolable in soft cypress-trees,
Etruscan cypresses.

Evil, what is evil?
There is only one evil, to deny life
As Rome denied Etruria
And mechanical America Montezuma still.

Fiesole.

Bat

At evening, sitting on this terrace,
When the sun from the west, beyond Pisa, beyond the mountains
    of Carrara
Departs, and the world is taken by surprise . . .

When the tired flower of Florence is in gloom beneath the
    glowing
Brown hills surrounding . . .

When under the arches of the Ponte Vecchio*
A green light enters against stream, flush from the west,
Against the current of obscure Arno . . .

Look up, and you see things flying
Between the day and the night;
Swallows with spools of dark thread sewing the shadows
    together.

A circle swoop, and a quick parabola under the bridge arches
Where light pushes through;
A sudden turning upon itself of a thing in the air.
A dip to the water.

And you think:
'The swallows are flying so late!'

Swallows?

Dark air-life looping
Yet missing the pure loop . . .
A twitch, a twitter, an elastic shudder in flight
And serrated wings against the sky,
Like a glove, a black glove thrown up at the light,
And falling back.

Never swallows!
Bats!
The swallows are gone.

At a wavering instant the swallows give way to bats
By the Ponte Vecchio . . .
Changing guard.

Bats, and an uneasy creeping in one's scalp
As the bats swoop overhead!
Flying madly.

Pipistrello!
Black piper on an infinitesimal pipe.
Little lumps that fly in air and have voices indefinite, wildly
      vindictive;

Wings like bits of umbrella.

Bats!

Creatures that hang themselves up like an old rag, to sleep;
And disgustingly upside down.
Hanging upside down like rows of disgusting old rags
And grinning in their sleep.
Bats!

In China the bat is symbol of happiness.

Not for me!

Snake

A snake came to my water-trough
On a hot, hot day, and I in pyjamas for the heat,
To drink there.

In the deep, strange-scented shade of the great dark carob-tree
I came down the steps with my pitcher
And must wait, must stand and wait, for there he was at the
    trough before me.

He reached down from a fissure in the earth-wall in the gloom
And trailed his yellow-brown slackness soft-bellied down, over
    the edge of the stone trough
And rested his throat upon the stone bottom,
And where the water had dripped from the tap, in a small
    clearness,
He sipped with his straight mouth,
Softly drank through his straight gums, into his slack long body,
Silently.

Someone was before me at my water-trough,
And I, like a second comer, waiting.

He lifted his head from his drinking, as cattle do,
And looked at me vaguely, as drinking cattle do,
And flickered his two-forked tongue from his lips, and mused a
    moment,
And stooped and drank a little more,
Being earth-brown, earth-golden from the burning bowels of the
    earth
On the day of Sicilian July, with Etna smoking.

The voice of my education said to me
He must be killed,
For in Sicily the black, black snakes are innocent, the gold are
    venomous.

And voices in me said, If you were a man
You would take a stick and break him now, and finish him off.

But must I confess how I liked him,
How glad I was he had come like a guest in quiet, to drink at my
      water-trough
And depart peaceful, pacified, and thankless,
Into the burning bowels of this earth?

Was it cowardice, that I dared not kill him?
Was it perversity, that I longed to talk to him?
Was it humility, to feel so honoured?
I felt so honoured.

And yet those voices:
If you were not afraid, you would kill him!

And truly I was afraid, I was most afraid,
But even so, honoured still more
That he should seek my hospitality
From out the dark door of the secret earth.

He drank enough
And lifted his head, dreamily, as one who has drunken,
And flickered his tongue like a forked night on the air, so black,
Seeming to lick his lips,
And looked around like a god, unseeing, into the air,
And slowly turned his head,
And slowly, very slowly, as if thrice adream,
Proceeded to draw his slow length curving round
And climb again the broken bank of my wall-face.

And as he put his head into that dreadful hole,
And as he slowly drew up, snake-easing his shoulders, and
      entered farther,
A sort of horror, a sort of protest against his withdrawing into
      that horrid black hole,
Deliberately going into the blackness, and slowly drawing himself
      after,
Overcame me now his back was turned.

I looked round, I put down my pitcher,
I picked up a clumsy log
And threw it at the water-trough with a clatter.

I think it did not hit him,
But suddenly that part of him that was left behind convulsed in
    undignified haste,
Writhed like lightning, and was gone
Into the black hole, the earth-lipped fissure in the wall-front,
At which, in the intense still noon, I stared with fascination.

And immediately I regretted it.
I thought how paltry, how vulgar, what a mean act!
I despised myself and the voices of my accursed human
    education.

And I thought of the albatross,
And I wished he would come back, my snake.

For he seemed to me again like a king,
Like a king in exile, uncrowned in the underworld,
Now due to be crowned again.

And so, I missed my chance with one of the lords
Of life.
And I have something to expiate;
A pettiness.

                                                    Taormina.

Baby Tortoise

You know what it is to be born alone,
Baby tortoise!

The first day to heave your feet little by little from the shell,
Not yet awake,
And remain lapsed on earth,
Not quite alive.

A tiny, fragile, half-animate bean.

To open your tiny beak-mouth, that looks as if it would never
　　　open,
Like some iron door;
To lift the upper hawk-beak from the lower base
And reach your skinny little neck
And take your first bite at some dim bit of herbage,
Alone, small insect,
Tiny bright-eye,
Slow one.

To take your first solitary bite
And move on your slow, solitary hunt.
Your bright, dark little eye,
Your eye of a dark disturbed night,
Under its slow lid, tiny baby tortoise,
So indomitable.

No one ever heard you complain.

You draw your head forward, slowly, from your little wimple
And set forward, slow-dragging, on your four-pinned toes,
Rowing slowly forward.
Whither away, small bird?
Rather like a baby working its limbs,

Except that you make slow, ageless progress
And a baby makes none.

The touch of sun excites you,
And the long ages, and the lingering chill
Make you pause to yawn,
Opening your impervious mouth,
Suddenly beak-shaped, and very wide, like some suddenly gaping
    pincers;
Soft red tongue, and hard thin gums,
Then close the wedge of your little mountain front,
Your face, baby tortoise.

Do you wonder at the world, as slowly you turn your head in its
    wimple
And look with laconic, black eyes?
Or is sleep coming over you again,
The non-life?

You are so hard to wake.

Are you able to wonder?
Or is it just your indomitable will and pride of the first life
Looking round
And slowly pitching itself against the inertia
Which had seemed invincible?

The vast inanimate,
And the fine brilliance of your so tiny eye,
Challenger.

Nay, tiny shell-bird,
What a huge vast inanimate it is, that you must row against,
What an incalculable inertia.

Challenger,
Little Ulysses, fore-runner,
No bigger than my thumb-nail,
Buon viaggio.

All animate creation on your shoulder,

Set forth, little Titan, under your battle-shield.

The ponderous, preponderate,
Inanimate universe;
And you are slowly moving, pioneer, you alone.

How vivid your travelling seems now, in the troubled sunshine,
Stoic, Ulyssean atom;
Suddenly hasty, reckless, on high toes.

Voiceless little bird,
Resting your head half out of your wimple
In the slow dignity of your eternal pause.
Alone, with no sense of being alone,
And hence six times more solitary;
Fulfilled of the slow passion of pitching through immemorial ages
Your little round house in the midst of chaos.

Over the garden earth,
Small bird,
Over the edge of all things.

Traveller,
With your tail tucked a little on one side
Like a gentleman in a long-skirted coat.

All life carried on your shoulder,
Invincible fore-runner.

Tortoise Shell

The Cross, the Cross
Goes deeper in than we know,
Deeper into life;
Right into the marrow
And through the bone.

Along the back of the baby tortoise
The scales are locked in an arch like a bridge,
Scale-lapping, like a lobster's sections
Or a bee's.

Then crossways down his sides
Tiger-stripes and wasp-bands.

Five, and five again, and five again,
And round the edges twenty-five little ones,
The sections of the baby tortoise shell.

Four, and a keystone;
Four, and a keystone;
Four, and a keystone;
Then twenty-four, and a tiny little keystone.

It needed Pythagoras to see life playing with counters on the
    living back
Of the baby tortoise;
Life establishing the first eternal mathematical tablet,
Not in stone, like the Judean Lord, or bronze, but in life-clouded,
    life-rosy tortoise shell.

The first little mathematical gentleman
Stepping, wee mite, in his loose trousers
Under all the eternal dome of mathematical law.

Fives, and tens,

Threes and fours and twelves,
All the *volte-face* of decimals,
The whirligig of dozens and the pinnacle of seven.

Turn him on his back,
The kicking little beetle,
And there again, on his shell-tender, earth-touching belly,
The long cleavage of division, upright of the eternal cross
And on either side count five,
On each side, two above, on each side, two below
The dark bar horizontal.

The Cross!
It goes right through him, the sprottling insect,
Through his cross-wise cloven psyche,
Through his five-fold complex-nature.

So turn him over on his toes again;
Four pin-point toes, and a problematical thumb-piece,
Four rowing limbs, and one wedge-balancing head,
Four and one makes five, which is the clue to all mathematics.

The Lord wrote it all down on the little slate
Of the baby tortoise.
Outward and visible indication of the plan within,
The complex, manifold involvedness of an individual creature
Plotted out
On this small bird, this rudiment,
This little dome, this pediment
Of all creation,
This slow one.

Tortoise Family Connections

On he goes, the little one,
Bud of the universe,
Pediment of life.

Setting off somewhere, apparently.
Whither away, brisk egg?

His mother deposited him on the soil as if he were no more than
    droppings,
And now he scuffles tinily past her as if she were an old rusty tin.

A mere obstacle,
He veers round the slow great mound of her –
Tortoises always foresee obstacles.

It is no use my saying to him in an emotional voice:
'This is your Mother, she laid you when you were an egg.'

He does not even trouble to answer: 'Woman, what have I to do
    with thee?'
He wearily looks the other way,
And she even more wearily looks another way still,
Each with the utmost apathy,
Incognisant,
Unaware,
Nothing.

As for papa,
He snaps when I offer him his offspring,
Just as he snaps when I poke a bit of stick at him,
Because he is irascible this morning, an irascible tortoise
Being touched with love, and devoid of fatherliness.

Father and mother,
And three little brothers,
And all rambling aimless, like little perambulating pebbles
    scattered in the garden,

Not knowing each other from bits of earth or old tins.

Except that papa and mama are old acquaintances, of course,
Though family feeling there is none, not even the beginnings.

Fatherless, motherless, brotherless, sisterless
Little tortoise.

Row on then, small pebble,
Over the clods of the autumn, wind-chilled sunshine,
Young gaiety.

Does he look for a companion?

No, no, don't think it.
He doesn't know he is alone;
Isolation is his birthright,
This atom.

To row forward, and reach himself tall on spiny toes,
To travel, to burrow into a little loose earth, afraid of the night,
To crop a little substance,
To move, and to be quite sure that he is moving:
Basta!
To be a tortoise!
Think of it, in a garden of inert clods
A brisk, brindled little tortoise, all to himself –
Adam!

In a garden of pebbles and insects
To roam, and feel the slow heart beat
Tortoise-wise, the first bell sounding
From the warm blood, in the dark-creation morning.

Moving, and being himself,
Slow, and unquestioned,
And inordinately there, O stoic!
Wandering in the slow triumph of his own existence,
Ringing the soundless bell of his presence in chaos,
And biting the frail grass arrogantly,
Decidedly arrogantly.

Tortoise Gallantry

Making his advances
He does not look at her, nor sniff at her,
No, not even sniff at her, his nose is blank.

Only he senses the vulnerable folds of skin
That work beneath her while she sprawls along
In her ungainly pace,
Her folds of skin that work and row
Beneath the earth-soiled hovel in which she moves.

And so he strains beneath her housey walls
And catches her trouser-legs in his beak
Suddenly, or her skinny limb,
And strange and grimly drags at her
Like a dog,
Only agelessly silent, with a reptile's awful persistency.

Grim, gruesome gallantry, to which he is doomed.
Dragged out of an eternity of silent isolation
And doomed to partiality, partial being,
Ache, and want of being,
Want,
Self-exposure, hard humiliation, need to add himself on to her.

Born to walk alone,
Fore-runner,
Now suddenly distracted into this mazy side-track,
This awkward, harrowing pursuit,
This grim necessity from within.

Does she know
As she moves eternally slowly away?
Or is he driven against her with a bang, like a bird flying in the
    dark against a window,
All knowledgeless?

The awful concussion,
And the still more awful need to persist, to follow, follow,
     continue,

Driven, after æons of pristine, fore-god-like singleness and
     oneness,
At the end of some mysterious, red-hot iron,
Driven away from himself into her tracks,
Forced to crash against her.

Stiff, gallant, irascible, crook-legged reptile,
Little gentleman,
Sorry plight,
We ought to look the other way.

Save that, having come with you so far,
We will go on to the end.

Humming-Bird

I can imagine, in some otherworld
Primeval-dumb, far back
In that most awful stillness, that only gasped and hummed,
Humming-birds raced down the avenues.

Before anything had a soul,
While life was a heave of Matter, half inanimate,
This little bit chipped off in brilliance
And went whizzing through the slow, vast, succulent stems.

I believe there were no flowers then,
In the world where the humming-bird flashed ahead of creation.
I believe he pierced the slow vegetable veins with his long beak.

Probably he was big
As mosses, and little lizards, they say, were once big.
Probably he was a jabbing, terrifying monster.

We look at him through the wrong end of the long telescope of
    Time,
Luckily for us.

Española.

She-Goat

Goats go past the back of the house like dry leaves in the dawn,
And up the hill like a river, if you watch.

At dusk they patter back like a bough being dragged on the
      ground,
Raising dusk and acridity of goats, and bleating.

Our old goat we tie up at night in the shed at the back of the
      broken Greek tomb in the garden,
And when the herd goes by at dawn she begins to bleat for me to
      come down and untie her.

Merr-err-err! Merr-er-errr! Mer! Mé!
— Wait, wait a bit, I'll come when I've lit the fire.
Merrr!
— Exactly.
Mé! Mer! Merrrrrrr!!!
*— Tace, tu, crapa, bestia!**
Merr-ererrr-ererrrr! Merrrr!

She is such an alert listener, with her ears wide, to know am I
      coming!
Such a canny listener, from a distance, looking upwards, lending
      first one ear, then another.

There she is, perched on her manger, looking over the boards
      into the day
Like a belle at her window.
And immediately she sees me she blinks, stares, doesn't know me,
      turns her head and ignores me vulgarly with a wooden blank
      on her face.

What do I care for her, the ugly female, standing up there with
      her long tangled sides like an old rug thrown over a fence.
But she puts her nose down shrewdly enough when the knot is
      untied,

And jumps staccato to earth, a sharp, dry jump, still ignoring me,
Pretending to look round the stall.

Come on, you crapa! I'm not your servant!

She turns her head away with an obtuse, female sort of deafness,
    bête.
And then invariably she crouches her rear and makes water.
That being her way of answer, if I speak to her. – Self-conscious!
Le bestie non parlano, poverine!

She was bought at Giardini fair, on the sands, for six hundred
    lire.

An obstinate old witch, almost jerking the rope from my hands to
    eat the acanthus, or bite at the almond buds, and make me
    wait.
Yet the moment I hate her she trips mild and smug like a woman
    going to mass.
The moment I really detest her.

Queer it is, suddenly, in the garden
To catch sight of her standing like some huge, ghoulish grey bird
    in the air, on the bough of the leaning almond-tree,
Straight as a board on the bough, looking down like some hairy
    horrid God the Father in a William Blake imagination.
Come down, crapa, out of that almond-tree!

Instead of which she strangely rears on her perch in the air, vast
    beast,
And strangely paws the air, delicate,
And reaches her black-striped face up like a snake, far up,
Subtly, to the twigs overhead, far up, vast beast,
And snaps them sharp, with a little twist of her anaconda head;
All her great hairy-shaggy belly open against the morning.

At seasons she curls back her tail like a green leaf in the fire,
Or like a lifted hand, hailing at her wrong end.
And having exposed the pink place of her nakedness, fixedly,

She trots on blithe toes,
And if you look at her, she looks back with a cold, sardonic stare.
Sardonic, sardonyx, rock of cold fire.
See me? She says, *That's me!*

That's her.

Then she leaps the rocks like a quick rock,
Her backbone sharp as a rock,
Sheer will.

Along which ridge of libidinous magnetism
Defiant, curling the leaf of her tail as if she were curling her lip
    behind her at all life,
Libidinous desire runs back and forth, asserting itself in that little
    lifted bare hand.

Yet she has such adorable spurty kids, like spurts of black ink.
And in a month again is as if she had never had them.

And when the billy goat mounts her
She is brittle as brimstone.
While his slitted eyes squint back to the roots of his ears.

Taormina.

Autumn at Taos

Over the rounded sides of the Rockies, the aspens of autumn,
The aspens of autumn,
Like yellow hair of a tigress brindled with pines.

Down on my hearth-rug of desert, sage of the mesa,
An ash-grey pelt
Of wolf all hairy and level, a wolf's wild pelt.

Trot-trot to the mottled foot-hills, cedar-mottled and pinon;
Did you ever see an otter?
Silvery-sided, fish-fanged, fierce-faced, whiskered, mottled.

When I trot my little pony through the aspen-trees of the canyon,
Behold me trotting at ease betwixt the slopes of the golden
Great and glistening-feathered legs of the hawk of Horus;
The golden hawk of Horus
Astride above me.

But under the pines
I go slowly
As under the hairy belly of a great black bear.

Glad to emerge and look back
On the yellow, pointed aspen-trees laid one on another like
    feathers,
Feather over feather on the breast of the great and golden
Hawk as I say of Horus.

Pleased to be out in the sage and the pine fish-dotted foot-hills,
Past the otter's whiskers,
On to the fur of the wolf-pelt that strews the plain.

And then to look back to the rounded sides of the squatting
    Rockies,
Tigress brindled with aspen,
Jaguar-splashed, puma-yellow, leopard-livid slopes of America.

Make big eyes, little pony,
At all these skins of wild beasts;
They won't hurt you.

Fangs and claws and talons and beaks and hawk-eyes
Are nerveless just now.
So be easy.

                                                        Taos.

Our Day is Over

Our day is over, night comes up
shadows steal out of the earth.
Shadows, shadows
wash over our knees and splash between our thighs,
our day is done;
we wade, we wade, we stagger, darkness rushes between our
        stones,
we shall drown.

Our day is over
night comes up.

How Beastly the Bourgeois is

How beastly the bourgeois is
especially the male of the species –

Presentable, eminently presentable –
shall I make you a present of him?

Isn't he handsome? Isn't he healthy? Isn't he a fine specimen?
Doesn't he look the fresh clean Englishman, outside?
Isn't it God's own image? tramping his thirty miles a day
after partridges, or a little rubber ball?
wouldn't you like to be like that, well off, and quite the thing?

Oh, but wait!
Let him meet a new emotion, let him be faced with another
    man's need,
let him come home to a bit of moral difficulty, let life face him
    with a new demand on his understanding
and then watch him go soggy, like a wet meringue.
Watch him turn into a mess, either a fool or a bully.
Just watch the display of him, confronted with a new demand on
    his intelligence,
a new life-demand.

How beastly the bourgeois is
especially the male of the species –

Nicely groomed, like a mushroom
standing there so sleek and erect and eyeable –
and like a fungus, living on the remains of bygone life
sucking his life out of the dead leaves of greater life than his own.

And even so, he's stale, he's been there too long.
Touch him, and you'll find he's all gone inside
just like an old mushroom, all wormy inside, and hollow
under a smooth skin and an upright appearance.

Full of seething, wormy, hollow feelings
rather nasty –
How beastly the bourgeois is!

Standing in their thousands, these appearances, in damp England
what a pity they can't all be kicked over
like sickening toadstools, and left to melt back, swiftly
into the soil of England.

Leda

Come not with kisses
not with caresses
of hands and lips and murmurings;
come with a hiss of wings
and sea-touch tip of a beak
and treading of wet, webbed, wave-working feet
into the marsh-soft belly.

A Living

A man should never earn his living,
if he earns his life he'll be lovely.

A bird
picks up its seeds or little snails
between heedless earth and heaven
in heedlessness.

But, the plucky little sport, it gives to life
song, and chirruping, gay feathers, fluff-shadowed warmth
and all the unspeakable charm of birds hopping and fluttering
    and being birds.
– And we, we get it all from them for nothing.

There is Rain in Me

There is rain in me
running down, running down, trickling
away from memory.

There is ocean in me
swaying, swaying O, so deep
so fathomlessly black
and spurting suddenly up, snow-white, like snow-leopards
　　　rearing
high and clawing with rage at the cliffs of the soul
then disappearing back with a hiss
of eternal salt rage; angry is old ocean within a man.

Man Reaches a Point

I cannot help but be alone
for desire has died in me, silence has grown,
and nothing now reaches out to draw
other flesh to my own.

Nemesis

The Nemesis that awaits our civilisation
is social insanity
which in the end is always homicidal.

Sanity means the wholeness of the consciousness.
And our society is only part conscious, like an idiot.

If we do not rapidly open all the doors of consciousness
and freshen the putrid little space in which we are cribbed
the sky-blue walls of our unventilated heaven
will be bright red with blood.

A Sane Revolution

If you make a revolution, make it for fun,
don't make it in ghastly seriousness,
don't do it in deadly earnest,
do it for fun.

Don't do it because you hate people,
do it just to spit in their eye.

Don't do it for the money,
do it and be damned to the money.

Don't do it for equality,
do it because we've got too much equality
and it would be fun to upset the apple-cart
and see which way the apples would go a-rolling.

Don't do it for the working classes.
Do it so that we can all of us be little aristocracies on our own
and kick our heels like jolly escaped asses.

Don't do it, anyhow, for international Labour.
Labour is the one thing a man has had too much of.
Let's abolish labour, let's have done with labouring!
Work can be fun, and men can enjoy it; then it's not labour.
Let's have it so! Let's make a revolution for fun!

Think—!

Imagine what it must have been to have existence
in the wild days when life was sliding whirlwinds, blue-hot
    weights,
in the days called chaos, which left us rocks, and gems!

Think that the sapphire is only alumina, like kitchen pans
crushed utterly, and breathed through and through
with fiery weight and wild life, and coming out
clear and flowery blue!

Trust

Oh we've got to trust
one another again
in some essentials.

Not the narrow little
bargaining trust
that says: I'm for you
if you'll be for me.

But a bigger trust,
a trust of the sun
that does not bother
about moth and rust,
and we see it shining
in one another.

Oh don't you trust me,
don't burden me
with your life and affairs; don't thrust me
into your cares.

But I think you may trust
the sun in me
that glows with just
as much glow as you see
in me, and no more.

But if it warms
your heart's quick core
why then trust it, it forms
one faithfulness more.

And be, oh be
a sun to me,
not a weary, insistent
personality

but a sun that shines
and goes dark, but shines
again and entwines
with the sunshine in me

till we both of us
are more glorious
and more sunny.

Andraitx* – Pomegranate Flowers

It is June, it is June
the pomegranates are in flower,
the peasants are bending cutting the bearded wheat.

The pomegranates are in flower
beside the high road, past the deathly dust,
and even the sea is silent in the sun.

Short gasps of flame in the green of night, way off
the pomegranates are in flower,
small sharp red fires in the night of leaves.

And noon is suddenly dark, is lustrous, is silent and dark
men are unseen, beneath the shading hats;
only, from out the foliage of the secret loins
red flamelets here and there reveal
a man, a woman there.

The Hostile Sun

Sometimes the sun turns hostile to men
when the daytime consciousness has got overweening
when thoughts are stiff, like old leaves
and ideas are hard, like acorns ready to fall.

Then the sun turns hostile to us
and bites at our throats and chests
as he bites at the stems of leaves in autumn, to make them fall.

Then we suffer, and though the sun bronzes us
we feel him strangling even more the issues of our soul
for he is hostile to all the old leafy foliage of our thoughts
and the old upward flowing of our sap, the pressure of our
    upward flow of feeling
is against him.

Then only under the moon, cool and unconcerned
calm with the calm of scimitars and brilliant reaping hooks
sweeping the curve of space and moving the silence
we have peace.

The Triumph of the Machine

They talk of the triumph of the machine,
but the machine will never triumph.

Out of the thousands and thousands of centuries of man
the unrolling of ferns, white tongues of the acanthus lapping at
    the sun,
for one sad century
machines have triumphed, rolled us hither and thither,
shaking the lark's nest till the eggs have broken.

Shaken the marshes till the geese have gone
and the wild swans flown away singing the swan-song of us.

Hard, hard on the earth the machines are rolling,
but through some hearts they will never roll.

The lark nests in his heart
and the white swan swims in the marshes of his loins,
and through the wide prairies of his breast a young bull herds the
    cows,
lambs frisk among the daisies of his brain.

And at last
all these creatures that cannot die, driven back
into the uttermost corners of the soul
will send up the wild cry of despair.

The trilling lark in a wild despair will trill down from the sky,
the swan will beat the waters in rage, white rage of an enraged
    swan,
even the lambs will stretch forth their necks like serpents,
like snakes of hate, against the man in the machine:
even the shaking white poplar will dazzle like splinters of glass
    against him.

And against this inward revolt of the native creatures of the soul
mechanical man, in triumph seated upon the seat of his machine
will be powerless, for no engine can reach into the marshes and
    depths of a man.

So mechanical man in triumph seated upon the seat of his
    machine
will be driven mad from himself, and sightless, and on that day
the machines will turn to run into one another
traffic will tangle up in a long-drawn-out crash of collision
and engines will rush at the solid houses, the edifice of our life
will rock in the shock of the mad machine, and the house will
    come down.

Then, far beyond the ruin, in the far, in the ultimate, remote
    places
the swan will lift up again his flattened, smitten head
and look round, and rise, and on the great vaults of his wings
will sweep round and up to greet the sun with a silky glitter of a
    new day
and the lark will follow trilling, angerless again,
and the lambs will bite off the heads of the daisies for friskiness.
But over the middle of the earth will be the smoky ruin of iron
the triumph of the machine.

Dark Satanic Mills

The dark, satanic mills of Blake
how much darker and more satanic they are now!
But oh, the streams that stream white-faced, in and out
in and out when the hooter hoots, whitefaced, with a dreadful
    gush
of multitudinous ignominy,
what shall we think of these?
They are millions to my one!

They are millions to my one! But oh
what have they done to you, white-faced millions
mewed and mangled in the mills of man?
What have they done to you, what have they done to you,
what is this awful aspect of man?

Oh Jesus, didn't you see, when you talked of service
this would be the result!
When you said: Retro me, Satanas!*
this is what you gave him leave to do
behind your back!

And now, the iron has entered into the soul
and the machine has entangled the brain, and got it fast,
and steel has twisted the loins of man, electricity has exploded
    the heart
and out of the lips of people just strange mechanical noises in
    place of speech.

What is man, that thou art no longer mindful of him!
and the son of man, that thou pitiest him not?
Are these no longer men, these millions, millions?
What are they then?

We Die Together

Oh, when I think of the industrial millions, when I see some of
    them,
a weight comes over me heavier than leaden linings of coffins
and I almost cease to exist, weighed down to extinction
and sunk into depression that almost blots me out.

Then I say to myself: Am I also dead? is that the truth?
Then I know
that with so many dead men in mills
I too am almost dead.
I know the unliving factory-hand, living-dead millions
is unliving me, living-dead me,
I, with them, am living dead, mechanical enslaved at the
    machine.

And enshrouded in the vast corpse of the industrial millions
embedded in them, I look out on the sunshine of the South.

And though the pomegranate has red flowers outside the window
and oleander is hot with perfume under the afternoon sun
and I am «Il Signore» and they love me here,
yet I am a mill-hand in Leeds
and the death of the Black Country is upon me
and I am wrapped in the lead of a coffin-lining, the living death of
    my fellow men.

Trees in the Garden

Ah in the thunder air
how still the trees are!

And the lime-tree, lovely and tall, every leaf silent
hardly looses even a last breath of perfume.

And the ghostly, creamy coloured little tree of leaves
white, ivory white among the rambling greens
how evanescent, variegated elder, she hesitates on the green
    grass
as if, in another moment, she would disappear
with all her grace of foam!

And the larch that is only a column, it goes up too tall to see:
and the balsam-pines that are blue with the grey-blue
    blueness of things from the sea,
and the young copper beach, its leaves red-rosy at the ends
how still they are together, they stand so still
in the thunder air, all strangers to one another
as the green grass glows upwards, strangers in the garden.

Lichtental.

Storm in the Black Forest

Now it is almost night, from the bronzey soft sky
jugfull after jugfull of pure white liquid fire, bright white
tipples over and spills down,
and is gone
and gold-bronze flutters beat through the thick upper air.

And as the electric liquid pours out, sometimes
a still brighter white snake wriggles among it, spilled
and tumbling wriggling down the sky:
and then the heavens cackle with uncouth sounds.

And the rain won't come, the rain refuses to come!

This is the electricity that man is supposed to have mastered
chained, subjugated to his use!
supposed to!

Service

Ah yes, men must learn to serve
not for money, but for life.

Ah yes, men must learn to obey
not a boss, but the gleam of life on the face of a man
who has looked into the eyes of the gods.

Man is only perfectly human
when he looks beyond humanity.

The Gods! The Gods!

People were bathing and posturing themselves on the beach
and all was dreary, great robot limbs, robot breasts
robot voices, robot even the gay umbrellas.

But a woman, shy and alone, was washing herself under a tap
and the glimmer of the presence of the gods was like lilies,
and like water-lilies.

The English are So Nice!

The English are so nice
so awfully nice
they are the nicest people in the world.

And what's more, they're very nice about being nice
about your being nice as well!
If you're not nice they soon make you feel it.

Americans and French and Germans and so on
they're all very well
but they're not *really* nice, you know.
They're not nice in *our* sense of the word, are they now?

That's why one doesn't have to take them seriously.
We must be nice to them, of course,   ·
of course, naturally.
But it doesn't really matter what you say to them,
they don't really understand
you can just say anything to them:
be nice, you know, just nice
but you must never take them seriously, they wouldn't
     understand,
just be nice, you know! oh, fairly nice,
not too nice of course, they take advantage
but nice enough, just nice enough
to let them feel they're not quiet as nice as they might be.

Travel is Over

I have travelled, and looked at the world, and loved it.
Now I don't want to look at the world any more,
there seems nothing there.
In not-looking, and in not-seeing
comes a new strength
and undeniable new gods share their life with us, when we cease
    to see.

For a Moment

For a moment, at evening, tired, as he stepped off the tram-car,
– the young tram-conductor in a blue uniform, to himself
      forgotten, –
and lifted his face up, with blue eyes looking at the electric rod
      which he was going to turn round,
for a moment, pure in the yellow evening light, he was
      Hyacinthus.

In the green garden darkened the shadow of coming rain
and a girl ran swiftly, laughing breathless, taking in her white
      washing
in rapid armfuls from the line, tossing in the basket,
and so rapidly, and so flashing, fleeing before the rain
for a moment she was Io, Io, who fled from Zeus, or the Danae.

When I was waiting and not thinking, sitting at a table on the
      hotel terrace
I saw suddenly coming towards me, lit up and uplifted with
      pleasure
advancing with the slow-swiftness of a ship backing her white
      sails into port
the woman who looks for me in the world
and for the moment she was Isis, gleaming, having found her
      Osiris.

For a moment, as he looked at me through his spectacles
pondering, yet eager, the broad and thick-set Italian who works
      in with me,
for a moment he was the Centaur, the wise yet horse-hoofed
      Centaur,
in whom I can trust.

God is Born

The history of the cosmos
is the history of the struggle of becoming.
When the dim flux of unformed life
struggled, convulsed back and forth upon itself,
and broke at last into light and dark
came into existence as light,
came into existence as cold shadow
then every atom of the cosmos trembled with delight.
Behold, God is born!
He is bright light!
He is pitch dark and cold!

And in the great struggle of intangible chaos
when, at a certain point, a drop of water began to drip
        downwards
and a breath of vapour began to wreath up
Lo again the shudder of bliss through all the atoms!
Oh, God is born!
Behold, he is born wet!
Look, He hath movement upward! He spirals!

And so, in the great aeons of accomplishment and débacle
from time to time the wild crying of every electron:
Lo! God is born

When sapphires cooled out of molten chaos:
See, God is born! He is blue, he is deep blue, he is for ever blue!
When gold lay shining threading the cooled-off rock:
God is born! God is born! bright yellow and ductile He is born.

When the little eggy amoeba emerged out of foam and nowhere
then all the electrons held their breath:
Ach! Ach! Now indeed God is born! He twinkles within.

When from a world of mosses and of ferns

at last the narcissus lifted a tuft of five-point stars
and dangled them in the atmosphere,
then every molecule of creation jumped and clapped its hands:
God is born! God is born perfumed and dangling and with a little
    cup!

Throughout the aeons, as the lizard swirls his tail finer than
    water,
as the peacock turns to the sun, and could not be more splendid,
as the leopard smites the small calf with a spangled paw, perfect,
the universe trembles: God is born! God is here!

And when at last man stood on two legs and wondered,
then there was a hush of suspense at the core of every electron:
Behold, now very God is born!
God Himself is born!
And so we see, God is not
until he is born.

And also we see
there is no end to the birth of God.

The Rainbow

Even the rainbow has a body
made of the drizzling rain
and is an architecture of glistening atoms
built up, built up
yet you can't lay your hand on it,
nay, nor even your mind.

The Man of Tyre

The man of Tyre went down to the sea
pondering, for he was Greek, that God is one and all alone and
    ever more shall be so.

And a woman who had been washing clothes in the pool of rock
where a stream came down to the gravel of the sea and sank in,
who had spread white washing on the gravel banked above the
    bay,
who had lain her shift on the shore, on the shingle slope,
who had waded to the pale green sea of evening, out to a shoal,
pouring sea-water over herself
now turned, and came slowly back, with her back to the evening
    sky.

Oh lovely, lovely with the dark hair piled up, as she went deeper,
    deeper down the channel, then rose shallower, shallower,
with the full thighs slowly lifting of the wader wading shorewards
and the shoulders pallid with light from the silent sky behind
both breasts dim and mysterious, with the glamorous kindness of
    twilight between them
and the dim blotch of black maidenhair like an indicator,
giving a message to the man –

So in the cane-brake he clasped his hands in delight
that could only be god-given, and murmured:
Lo! God is one god! But here in the twilight
godly and lovely comes Aphrodite out of the sea
    towards me!

They Say the Sea is Loveless

They say the sea is loveless, that in the sea
love cannot live, but only bare, salt splinters
of loveless life.
But from the sea
the dolphins leap round Dionysos' ship
whose masts have purple vines,
and up they come with the purple dark of rainbows
and flip! they go! with the nose-dive of sheer delight;
and the sea is making love to Dionysos
in the bouncing of these small and happy whales.

Bavarian Gentians

Not every man has gentians in his house
in Soft September, at slow, Sad Michaelmas.

Bavarian gentians, big and dark, only dark
darkening the day-time torch-like with the smoking blueness of
    Pluto's gloom,
ribbed and torch-like, with their blaze of darkness spread blue
down flattening into points, flattened under the sweep of white
    day
torch-flower of the blue-smoking darkness, Pluto's dark-blue
    daze,
black lamps from the halls of Dio, burning dark blue,
giving off darkness, blue darkness, as Demeter's pale lamps give
    off light,
lead me then, lead me the way.

Reach me a gentian, give me a torch!
let me guide myself with the blue, forked torch of this flower
down the darker and darker stairs, where blue is darkened on
    blueness
even where Persephone goes, just now, from the frosted
    September
to the sightless realm where darkness is awake upon the dark
and Persephone herself is but a voice
or a darkness invisible enfolded in the deeper dark
of the arms Plutonic, and pierced with the passion of dense
    gloom,
among the splendour of torches of darkness, shedding darkness
    on the lost bride and her groom.

Lucifer

Angels are bright still, though the brightest fell.
But tell me, tell me, how do you know
he lost any of his brightness in the falling?
In the dark-blue depths, under layers and layers of darkness
I see him more like the ruby, a gleam from within
of his own magnificence
coming like the ruby in the invisible dark, glowing
with his own annunciation, towards us.

The Breath of Life

The breath of life is in the sharp winds of change
mingled with the breath of destruction.
But if you want to breathe deep, sumptuous life
breathe all alone, in silence, in the dark,
and see nothing.

Mana of the Sea

Do you see the sea, breaking itself to bits against the islands
yet remaining unbroken, the level great sea?

Have I caught from it
the tide in my arms
that runs down to the shallows of my wrists, and breaks
abroad in my hands, like waves among the rocks of substance?

Do the rollers of the sea
roll down my thighs
and over the submerged islets of my knees
with power, sea-power
sea-power
to break against the ground
in the flat, recurrent breakers of my two feet?

And is my body ocean, ocean
whose power runs to the shores along my arms
and breaks in the foamy hands, whose power rolls out
to the white-treading waves of two salt feet?

I am the sea, I am the sea!

The Ship of Death

Now it is autumn and the falling fruit
and the long journey towards oblivion.

The apples falling like great drops of dew
to bruise themselves an exit from themselves.

And it is time to go, to bid farewell
to one's own self, and find an exit
from the fallen self.

II

Have you built your ship of death, O have you?
O build your ship of death, for you will need it.

The grim frost is at hand, when the apples will fall
thick, almost thundrous, on the hardened earth.

And death is on the air like a smell of ashes!
Ah! can't you smell it?
And in the bruised body, the frightened soul
finds itself shrinking, wincing from the cold
that blows upon it through the orifices.

III

And can a man his own quietus make
with a bare bodkin?

With daggers, bodkins, bullets, man can make
a bruise or break of exit for his life;
but is that a quietus, O tell me, is it quietus?

Surely not so! for how could murder, even self-murder
ever a quietus make?

IV

O let us talk of quiet that we know,
that we can know, the deep and lovely quiet
of a strong heart at peace!

How can we this, our own quietus, make?

V

Build then the ship of death, for you must take
the longest journey, to oblivion.

And die the death, the long and painful death
that lies between the old self and the new.

Already our bodies are fallen, bruised, badly bruised,
already our souls are oozing through the exit
of the cruel bruise.

Already the dark and endless ocean of the end
is washing in through the breaches of our wounds,
already the flood is upon us.

Oh build your ship of death, your little ark
and furnish it with food, with little cakes, and wine
for the dark flight down oblivion.

VI

Piecemeal the body dies, and the timid soul
has her footing washed away, as the dark flood rises.

We are dying, we are dying, we are all of us dying
and nothing will stay the death-flood rising within us
and soon it will rise on the world, on the outside world.

We are dying, we are dying, piecemeal our bodies are dying
and our strength leaves us,
and our soul cowers naked in the dark rain over the flood,
cowering in the last branches of the tree of our life.

VII

We are dying, we are dying, so all we can do
is now to be willing to die, and to build the ship
of death to carry the soul on the longest journey.

A little ship, with oars and food
and little dishes, and all accoutrements
fitting and ready for the departing soul.

Now launch the small ship, now as the body dies
and life departs, launch out, the fragile soul
in the fragile ship of courage, the ark of faith
with its store of food and little cooking pans
and change of clothes,
upon the flood's black waste
upon the waters of the end
upon the sea of death, where still we sail
darkly, for we cannot steer, and have no port.

There is no port, there is nowhere to go
only the deepening blackness darkening still
blacker upon the soundless, ungurgling flood
darkness at one with darkness, up and down
and sideways utterly dark, so there is no direction any more.
and the little ship is there; yet she is gone.
She is not seen, for there is nothing to see her by.
She is gone! gone! and yet
somewhere she is there.
Nowhere!

VIII

And everything is gone, the body is gone
completely under, gone, entirely gone.
The upper darkness is heavy as the lower,
between them the little ship
is gone

It is the end, it is oblivion.

IX

And yet out of eternity a thread
separates itself on the blackness,
a horizontal thread
that fumes a little with pallor upon the dark.

Is it illusion? or does the pallor fume
A little higher?
Ah wait, wait, for there's the dawn,
the cruel dawn of coming back to life
out of oblivion.

Wait, wait, the little ship
drifting, beneath the deathly ashy grey
of a flood-dawn.

Wait, wait! even so, a flush of yellow
and strangely, O chilled wan soul, a flush of rose.

A flush of rose, and the whole thing starts again.

X

The flood subsides, and the body, like a worn sea-shell
emerges strange and lovely.
And the little ship wings home, faltering and lapsing
on the pink flood,
and the frail soul steps out, into the house again
filling the heart with peace.

Swings the heart renewed with peace
even of oblivion.

Oh build your ship of death. Oh build it!
for you will need it.
For the voyage of oblivion awaits you.

Sleep and Waking

In sleep I am not, I am gone
I am given up.
And nothing in the world is lovelier than sleep,
dark, dreamless sleep, in deep oblivion!
Nothing in life is quite so good as this.

Yet there is waking from the soundest sleep,
waking, and waking new.

Did you sleep well?
Ah yes, the sleep of God!
The world is created afresh.

Shadows

And if tonight my soul may find her peace
in sleep, and sink in good oblivion,
and in the morning wake like a new-opened flower
then I have been dipped again in God, and new-created.

And if, as weeks go round, in the dark of the moon
my spirit darkens and goes out, and soft strange gloom
pervades my movements and my thoughts and words
then I shall know that I am walking still
with God, we are close together now the moon's in shadow.

And if, as autumn deepens and darkens
I feel the pain of falling leaves, and stems that break in storms
and trouble and dissolution and distress
and then the softness of deep shadows folding, folding
around my soul and spirit, around my lips
so sweet, like a swoon, or more like the drowse of a low, sad song
singing darker than the nightingale, on, on to the solstice
and the silence of short days, the silence of the year, the shadow,
then I shall know that my life is moving still
with the dark earth, and drenched
with the deep oblivion of earth's lapse and renewal.

And if, in the changing phases of man's life
I fall in sickness and in misery
my wrists seem broken and my heart seems dead
and strength is gone, and my life
is only the leavings of a life:

and still, among it all, snatches of lovely oblivion, and snatches of
     renewal
odd, wintry flowers upon the withered stem, yet new, strange
     flowers
such as my life has not brought forth before, new blossoms of
     me—

then I must know that still
I am in the hands of the unknown God,
he is breaking me down to his own oblivion
to send me forth on a new morning, a new man.

Phoenix

Are you willing to be sponged out, erased, cancelled,
made nothing?
Are you willing to be made nothing?
dipped into oblivion?

If not, you will never really change.

The phoenix renews her youth
only when she is burnt, burnt alive, burnt down
to hot and flocculent ash.
Then the small stirring of a new small bub in the nest
with strands of down like floating ash
Shows that she is renewing her youth like the eagle
Immortal bird.

Notes

pp. 9 Corot Jean-Baptiste Corot (1796–1875). French landscape painter, admired and copied by Lawrence. Copying paintings was a hobby of Lawrence's in the years just before the Great War.

p. 32 Giorno dei Morti Day of the Dead in Italy, 2 November.

p. 41 Bat the Ponte Vecchio is the oldest bridge across the River Arno in Florence.

p. 56 She-Goat *'Tace, tu, crapa, bestia.'* Italian (in the dialect of Sicily), meaning 'shut-up, you she-goat animal'.

p. 73 Andraitx a town on Majorca, where Lawrence stayed in the summer of 1929.

p. 77 Dark Satanic Mills *'Retro me, Satanas!'* (Latin): 'Get thee behind me Satan.' Matthew 16:23, Mark 8:33, Luke 4:8.